The Lakeland C

Published March 2007 by P3 Publi

ISBN 978-0-9547739-6-0

Contributors

The publisher would like to thank the members of the Lake District Osprey Project for agreeing to the publishing of this book and for facilitating access to the information and pictures necessary to do so. The photographs have been mainly supplied by the Lake District Osprey Project, as well as the RSPB and several individuals. Individual credits can be found beside each image. Finally I would like to thank, in particular, Pete Barron of the Lake District National Park Authority and Pete Davies for their liasion role. Their co-operation with the provision of resource material and critical advice has helped me enormously and made the task of producing this book much easier than I first anticipated.

David Ramshaw
Publisher & Author

Mike Moore

Printed and bound in Great Britain by
Amadeus Press
Cleckheaton
BD19 4TQ

Published by P3 Publications
13 Beaver Road
Carlisle
CA2 7PS
www.p3publications.com

The Lakeland Ospreys

This book describes the story of the arrival of ospreys at Bassenthwaite in 1997, through to the first breeding the Lake District has recorded in 2001, and tells the fascinating life cycle of the ospreys through the breeding seasons.

Contents

The Lakeland Ospreys

Osprey Facts

The osprey is found on all continents except Antartica.

The word 'osprey' was first mentioned in its Latin form 'Ossifrage' by Pliny and probably referred to a bearded vulture or Lammergeier. It was allegedly first used for the species that we know as **Pandion Haliaetus** by Turner in 1544. It also appeared in early literature such as *'The Battle of Alcazar'* (1594) and *'The Song of Lincolnshire'* (1613). It was in these early writings that a superstition arose that the osprey had a fabulous power which attracted fish into the upper waters.

There are four sub-species of osprey - *Pandion haliaetus*.
Origin of name: ***Pandion*** after the mythical king of Athens, ***haliaetus*** from the Greek ***hals*** and ***aetus*** for 'sea' and 'eagle'.

The sub-species are:

1.   ***P h haliaetus*** - found in Scotland (and now England and Wales) and mainland Eurasia. The territory extends east to Kamchatka and Japan, south locally to Cape Verdes, the Mediterranean, the Red Sea, the Persian Gulf, the Himalaya, Southeast China and Taiwan. Migratory

2.   ***P h carolinensis*** - N America south to Florida and Mexican Gulf of California. Migratory

3.   ***P h ridgwayi*** - Bahamas, Cuban cays, Yucatan and Belize. Non-migratory

4.   ***P h cristatus*** - Sulawesi and Java east to Solomons and New Caledonia and south to coastal Australia. Non-migratory

Chris Gomersall / rspb-images.com

Osprey Facts *(continued)*

	Male	Female
Length	53-63 cm	53-63 cm
Wing	45-50 cm	47-52 cm
Tail	17-21 cm	19.5-24 cm
Wingspan	146-173 cm	146-173 cm
Weight	1.12 - 1.74 Kg	1.21-2.05 kg

R Wahl

Female ospreys are 3% to 4% larger than the male and are 14% heavier.

Fishing

The average prey is almost entirely live fish, freshwater or salt, surface-swimming species. The typical **weight** of a catch is 250g. Birds have been recorded catching species from 200g up to 1500g! The actual **size** of a catch on average is *25-35* cms. Examples have been recorded from 7cm to 57cms.

Ospreys have been recorded with non-fish prey, such as snakes, aquatic mammals, voles, squirrels, small alligators, conchs and even birds.

The table at the bottom of the next page shows the percentage of different fish species caught by the Bassenthwaite ospreys from 2004 to 2006.

Frequency of feeding: according to literature, during incubation the male bird brings fish to the female on average *1.7-1.8* times per day. In 2003 during incubation the Bassenthwaite male averaged *2.6* times per day. Once the chicks have hatched he has been recorded carrying fish to the nest as follows: to a nest with two chicks *3.6* times per day and to a nest with three chicks *4.6* times per day.

Migration: on their migration flights ospreys catch approximately two fish per day and require a total of approx. 500g of fish per day. The osprey has heavy **tarsi** (ankle bones) with large feet, reversible outer toes, long curved claws and spiny

The Lakeland Ospreys

soles. These are all adaptations for grasping slippery prey. The osprey is the only raptor with these reversible toes. After catching a fish they usually turn it head forwards to improve the aerodynamics (see fish catching sequence on page 16).

Eggs: a clutch normally consists of two to three eggs, but clutches of both one and four eggs have been recorded. Eggs are usully laid at intervals of one to two days, with the last egg being smaller and lighter than the first.
The eggs weigh between *68-71 g* and measure *62 x 46 mm* approximately.

Incubation: the birds sit on the eggs for an average of 37 days, the range is between 34 and 40 days.

Osprey foot showing reversible outer toe

Hatching: the eggs hatch at intervals, normally at least a day, in the order that they were laid, so that initially chicks will be different sizes. A good fish supply from the male helps them to thrive and survive - osprey chicks don't show the same antagonism towards each other as do owl and other raptor species.

Fledging: the birds begin to fly on average 53 days after hatching, the range is between 49 and 57 days. Studies have shown that they become independent of their parents from 30 days after learning to fly.

Survival: there is up to 70% mortality rate of juveniles in their first year of life. However 85-90% of breeding adults survive each year. The oldest recorded age for an osprey is 32 years.

Nest: a typical osprey nest is between 1.2 and 1.5 metres in width and between 50cm and two metres deep. It can be the size of a double bed!

Fish species as caught by the Bassenthwaite ospreys			
Fish Species	**2004 (%)**	**2005 (%)**	**2006 (%)**
Perch	43.5	38.5	40
Pike	1.5	4	4
Trout	9	23.5	17
Roach	6	3.5	6
Bream	0.5	0.5	0.5
Dace	0.5	0	6
Rudd	1	3	0.5
Salmon	0	0	3
Unidentified	38	27.5	23

The Lakeland Ospreys

History of osprey breeding in Great Britain.

Until recent years one had to go back to 1676, at Whinfield Park, and 1831, at Corby Castle for records of breeding ospreys in Cumbria. Ospreys ceased breeding in England (Somerset) in 1842. In Britain the last known pair to breed prior to extinction was in Invernessshire in 1916. Extinction was unfortunately caused by human persecution. Adults were shot for their skins and eggs were stolen for collections. Surprisingly, there is no evidence that ospreys have ever bred in the Lake District and certainly not for the last 150 years. Historical records often confuse them with white-tailed sea eagles, as both species take fish from the water.

This puts the events of 2001 in some perspective, the first ever confirmed breeding of ospreys in the Lake District and the start of the natural recolonisation of England.

Throughout the period from 1916 onwards there were ospreys passing through river valleys of Cumbria on passage. It is now generally recognised that ospreys did breed (more or less undetected) in Scotland between 1916 and the well documented return to the Loch Garten area in 1954 when a pair bred successfully on Speyside, but nest robbery stopped further success until 1959 when the RSPB opened the now famous Loch Garten site for public viewing. This site has had a breeding pair every year since.

This was quite an achievement. George Waterson, the then RSPB Director for Scotland, took a very brave, far-sighted decision and opened up the Loch Garten site to the public, 14,000 of whom watched these amazing birds in their first year. The principle of gaining public support en masse for conservation measures may well have been born at an osprey nest.

Artificial nest building at Bassenthwaite

The Lakeland Ospreys

Lakeland perspective and history

In the Lake District summering birds had been observed in favoured locations but, in 1997, a pair stayed at Bassenthwaite Lake for a short summer and returned for a full summer in 1998 (One of the birds had a green ring attached. For further details on osprey ringing see pages 30 and 31). They had obviously decided it was not a bad place to stay, as they returned in 1999.

It was in 1998 that the idea of nest provision came to fruition, and it was decided to build a number of artificial nest sites. Mating was observed on one of the nest sites in May 2000 (the favourite one according to LDOP members), so things looked good. At this time very few people were aware of these events so 2001 was awaited eagerly.

Even fewer people knew that in 1999 a significant event occurred elsewhere in Cumbria, which was kept secret at the time. A pair of ospreys were found with a nest, which failed at the egg stage. These birds returned in 2000 and successfully reared a single chick, the **FIRST** in Cumbria for at least 170 years and the first recorded in **ENGLAND** since 1842. The same birds returned in 2001 and reared three chicks. There were two such sites that were kept secret. However there was suspicion of persecution at the second secret site, in this and in subsequent years. Unfortunately both of these sites are now unoccupied.

It was in the winter of 2000 that the **Lake District Osprey Project** was formed with forward planning for potential breeding. The project brought together three organisations, The Lake District National Park Authority, The Forestry Commission and the RSPB.

Sure enough the birds returned in April 2001 and incubation began, as did the start of their protection. This was, of course, the year that Foot and Mouth Disease ravaged Britain, and northern Cumbria in particular. This was both an advantage and a disadvantage. On the positive side, staff were released from other duties and showed tremendous dedication, concentrating for long hours, often in the freezing cold, watching out for unwanted intruders.

All were kept going by the will to protect these special birds from egg collectors. The Cumbria Constabulary also gave vital and enthusiastic back up. On the negative side Foot and Mouth Disease had got a firm grip by April and caused problems of access at the best watch points. However, a suitable *viewing hole* was found and great discretion was exercised

The Lakeland Ospreys

on arriving and leaving. Then, on 13 June 2001 the first osprey recorded in Lake District history hatched. Bassenthwaite reared a single chick (seen on the front cover). Including the other secret site, a total of 14 chicks have flown from Cumbria between the years 2000 and 2006

Bassenthwaite - Pre-breeding and History

Records of passage birds within the breeding season have increased over recent years and include two juvenile ospreys which stayed at Bassenthwaite for a short time in the summer of 1997. In 1998 two birds again graced the lake, arriving in mid April and staying until 17 August. One of the birds had been ringed as a nestling on Speyside in July 1995 (a green ring SX) and gave a good indication of the plumage state of a three year old bird. It is believed that this was the first sighting of the female that has returned to Bassenthwaite ever since.

It was at this point that the possibility of ospreys breeding at Bassenthwaite became apparent, although the pessimists of this world gave it no chance, since other locations had had summering juveniles which had come to nothing, the young birds apparently tending to return to their natal area to breed.

However, Pete Barron, of the Lake District National Park Authority, had a prophecy, '*ringing in his ears*', that he had read in a book by Roy Dennis (Highland Foundation for Wildlife). This stated that once Scottish breeding numbers had gone over the 100 pairs mark, the spread into England was a strong possibility. Roy was to be proved right, but not for a further two years.

Currently (2006) there are over 180 breeding pairs of ospreys in Scotland.

'It was necessary to set up a 24 hour watch of the nest site'

A juvenile osprey

The Lakeland Ospreys

The finished nest

Pete Barron had identified one major problem, a lack of flat topped, old Scots pines, so favoured by ospreys in Scotland for constructing their huge stick nests. The "pointy topped" spruces, firs and oaks in the area were not exactly ideal. Pete contacted Graeme Prest, the local Forestry Commission manager, and a keen birder, who had worked with ospreys in the Highlands.

In July 1998 the Lake District National Park Authority and the Forestry Commission got together to scour the woods for suitable, secluded locations, where they put up a number of nest platforms. This entailed cutting the top out of a suitable tree and placing a frame of timber on which branches and twigs were added to make an artificial nest nearly two metres wide! Ospreys like to think that others have been there before, and will more readily choose a previously used site, so each winter the team climbed the trees and splashed the "nests" with artificial guano (the cheapest white gloss). Nest platforms have been very successful worldwide so it was now fingers crossed and wait!

A camera mount is added

A pair once again summered from April to August 1999. Another winter of waiting and hoping ensued.

Then, the big breakthrough happened on 6 May 2000. Whilst bird ringing at Bassenthwaite, Pete Barron joked with a colleague, Pete Davies, that life would be complete if the ospreys were to use the platform.

The Lakeland Ospreys

Then ten minutes later it happened; the pair mating on the nest! More mating and stick gathering for the eyrie followed over the coming weeks. The male, however, seemed to be inexperienced, with much of the attempted mating often involving just standing on the back of the female. By 10 August both birds had departed southwards.

Bassenthwaite - 2000 Onwards

In the winter of 2000/01 planning was undertaken by a partnership of the Lake District National Park Authority, the Forestry Commission and the RSPB to jointly manage this historic turn of events; an ornithological development to which the project members were in no doubt would create interest locally and nationally.

This partnership became known as **'The Lake District Osprey Project'**

Mating on the nest

Stress levels began to build as news of the arrival of ospreys in Scotland came through in March and early April. Thoughts turned to what might have happened to the birds on their hazardous migration across desert and ocean.

Then on the 15th April the male was spotted at the Lake head, looking tired and preening on a favourite post. Just two days later, on the 17th April, his mate arrived and went straight to the nest, from which she rarely strayed until early August. There was a mixture of excitement and relief in the project team followed by:-

"we had better get a move on and get our plans into action!"

Favourite osprey posts

The ospreys (and the project team) immediately went into a frenzy of activity, the birds making numerous mating attempts, adding sticks and moss to the platform and the male displaying over the nest. Meanwhile the project team was dealing with the logistics of mounting a twenty four hour watch. One local farmer saw a large larch stick land in his farmyard, as the male prematurely dropped it on his way to the nest (this treasured stick now sits proudly on a mantelpiece)! The male's display, rarely witnessed in its full glory, but sensational to the lucky few, found him with a fish high in the sky and diving at break neck speed, pulling out of the dive, repeating the performance with a final power dive down to the nest to present his mate with a fish.

The First Egg (2001)

On 3 May, it is likely that the first egg was laid. The female does most of the incubating with the male giving her a break usually at dawn, bringing her a fish and allowing her to stretch her wings. Once laying was confirmed a round the clock watch was initiated with staff from all three partner organisations. With the continuing access restrictions due to foot and mouth disease, and there being no eagle viewpoint at Haweswater that season, a number of field staff were released from normal duties and showed tremendous dedication, concentrating for long hours, often in the freezing

Osprey carrying a stick

The male carrying a fish to his mate on the nest

'The female barely strayed from the nest until early August'

Carrying nest building material

11

cold, watching out for unwanted intruders. All were kept going by the will to protect these special birds from egg collectors. The local police also gave vital and reassuring back up.

It is doubtful if a more experienced full time crew will ever be gathered to do this work again and all involved must be thanked for their dedication, well above and beyond the norm, but then it was a unique situation.

The viewpoint at Dodd Wood

Plans were rapidly put into action for public viewing once the egg(s) hatched and the viewing platform at Dodd Wood was set up across the lake from the nest.

The first chick

Hatching was confirmed on 13 June when through the heat haze the adults could be seen feeding a chick deep in the nest, although it was not actually visible at this stage as it was so tiny. Elliot Morley, Forestry Minister, and keen birder, came to Bassenthwaite to officially announce the successful hatching and open the public viewpoint at Dodd Wood. The media came from London in force and the story made the national TV news, radio and newspapers. It was great to see Cumbria hitting the headlines with a good news story in the Foot and Mouth year.

The response to the news on the TV was immediate with members of the public arriving on the scene while the Minister and TV crews were still on site!

Mr Morley acted as *'viewpoint assistant'* showing people the birds through high-powered telescopes (provided by Viking Optics and Swarovski). This was almost certainly one of the Minister's more

The viewing platform at Dodd Wood

Elliot Morley with Tony Cunningham, local MP

The Lakeland Ospreys

A treasured photograph: the first chick, on the nest in 2001

The view from Dodd Wood to the nest site across the lake

pleasurable official engagements! The public interest was tremendous.

During the first weekend over 1600 visitors came and marvelled at a live wildlife spectacular of ospreys on the nest and the male fishing in the lake below and taking his prey to the nest. A team of partnership staff helped show people the birds - the project was off to a flying start! Over 25,000 people visited the viewpoint in just ten weeks! Visitors included keen birdwatchers from near and far, local people who have adopted the birds as their own, and holiday-makers of all ages for whom many this was their first wildlife viewing experience.

Hopefully this will have sparked a life long interest in wildlife and the environment among many, one of the most important aims of the project. Apart from stunning osprey action, Dodd Wood provides outstanding views across the fells, the lake, marshes and woodlands. There is a wealth of other wildlife to see, from red squirrels feeding at the viewpoint, to a family of foxes on the marshes, otters in the lake and buzzards overhead.

Overall it provides a wonderful opportunity to discuss nature conservation and the environment in this outdoor classroom.

The Lakeland Ospreys

A detailed account of the day to day life and habits of this osprey family at Bassenthwaite is given in a later chapter, '**The Osprey Year'**.

On 18 August, eight days after the chick had flown the nest, the female departed for Africa. The male and fledging stayed on until 15 September before departing, a late stay compared to other sites. During this time the male was seen catching and delivering fish to the young bird at the nest. Hopefully it would know how to do it itself in the near future.

Before fledging, the 2001 chick was ringed, a red ring numbered 15. Will Red 15 survive? As few as 30% of young birds survive their first year, but this rate of yearly survival increases to 90% by adulthood. Being a male, Red 15, all being well, will probably return to within ten kilometres of his natal area, Bassenthwaite Lake. Up to 2006 Red 15 had still not been sighted, but all concerned with the project are still looking.

Spring 2002 - *Return from migration*

The male returned on 3 April, the earliest date so far, but probably to be expected as previously successful breeders tend to return to the breeding grounds earlier than immature first time breeders. It was 0805 when he arrived. He paid a brief visit to the nest and then could be seen sitting in a tree by the river for much of the day, presumably recovering from the long migration. The male soon held territory over the nest site once again from the usual adversaries, buzzard, crow, raven, sparrowhawk and other raptors on occasions. He (and many others!) waited and waited for the female's return. The latest return date of 18 April

John Wright

Chris Gomersall / rspb-images.com

saw her travel up Borrowdale, arriving at Bassenthwaite in mid afternoon. She flew around the area, over the fellside at Barf, and interacted with the male, including a lot of calling before dropping onto the nest. Mating began almost immediately on the nest. This was followed by the male catching and, eventually, presenting the fish to the female.

Egg laying, incubation and hatching (2002)

On 3 May a new male appeared in the area and could be seen displaying over Dodd. This male caused confusion and concern for watchers as it was trying to win the attentions of the female with display and even brought fish to the nest. It may have been this confused situation which delayed egg laying as the first egg was not laid until 1400 on the 10 May. The first egg is usually laid twelve to fourteen days after mating.

The pair had been bringing in nest material including moss and it was in a deep scrape in the moss that the female laid and incubation began. Three eggs were eventually laid to make a normal full clutch for an osprey. Weather during the incubation period was shocking with very wet, windy, cool conditions and the birds had to sit tight. One of the eggs was broken, apparently stood on, possibly during one of the regular nest defences.

It was probably on the 17 June that the first egg hatched, with the second on the 19th. With the aid of the CCTV cameras, the young could be seen almost immediately.

(Continued on page 20)

The broken egg

2002 chicks on the nest

The Lakeland Ospreys

Ospreys Fishing

One of the most interesting attractions for visitors, when watching the ospreys from the viewpoint, is to observe them fishing. The series of pictures on the next two pages illustrates their technique. A fishing bird will fly high above the lake, descending to about 20 m in height when he sees a likely prey. The male, who is the main fish provider and most likely to be seen fishing, will hover at this height to fix on his target before stooping suddenly, straight into the water to catch the fish in his talons.

On his flight back to the nest he will turn the catch in his talons so that the head points forward, thus reducing the aerodynamic drag (or the wind resistance) on the fish.

Ospreys are almost exclusively fish eaters, but if mobbed by other birds, such as crows, they will very rarely lose their cool, attack, kill and eat one.

Mike Moore

1. The male hovering at about 20 m above the lake gets his eye on a suitable fish near the surface

LDOP

6. The osprey in the last picture has caught a young pike, much smaller than the one above. They often take pike but perch is their most usual catch

John Wright

9. A Rutland osprey breakfasting on a crow

LDOP

8. A roach - another common source of food for the osprey

LDOP

7. A perch - The most common prey of the Bassenthwaite ospreys

The Lakeland Ospreys

Chris Gomersall
rspb-images.com

2. A quick dive down to the water and he grabs the fish in his sharp talons

Mike Moore

3. He lifts the fish out of the water. In this case the fish has been caught with its head to the rear of the talons

Peter Cairns
rspb-images.com

5. He then flies back to a branch near the nest to eat, or prepare the fish for presenting to the female or chicks

Mike Moore

4. He now adjusts his grip on the fish so that its head is pointing forward, thus reducing air resistance on the fish

The Lakeland Ospreys

The Newly re-furbished Whinlatter Visitor Centre

Over £500,000 of grant funding was obtained to re-develop the Whinlatter Visitor Centre, including osprey interpretation and a giant video screen with live pictures beamed from the nest, and also to improve the visitor facilities at Dodd Wood. The main funders were European Union (ERDF), Rural Regeneration Cumbria, M-Sport and English Nature. Most of the funding was awarded so that we could capitalise on the benefits that the ospreys could bring to the local economy. The new Whinlatter centre was opened in spring 2003 by John Craven and the ospreys were featured on BBC Countryfile. The economic benefits have exceeded all expectations.

The temporary portakabins housing the CCTV displays in 2002

Ospreys and the local economy

An amazing 290,000 people visit osprey nest sites throughout Scotland, England and Wales each year. With such keen public interest in the birds themselves and the story of their remarkable recovery from near extinction, it is no surprise that ospreys, by attracting large numbers of visitors, provide major benefits to local economies.

A visitor survey in 2003 revealed that visitors to the Lake District ospreys spent a total of £1.68 million during their stay. Of this £420,000 can be attributed to the presence of the ospreys.

Portakabin with osprey nest outside

Inside, watching the ospreys

18

The Lakeland Ospreys

Volunteers

The osprey project has attracted over 70 volunteers working for the good of the ospreys. They are the backbone of the project. Without their precious gift of time, skills, enthusiasm and experience the project simply could not operate. Volunteers are involved in all aspects of the project; enthusing the public, manning the round the clock nest watch, fundraising and much more. In 2006, volunteers gave over 6000 hours of their time to the ospreys. This was a remarkable achievement, that was recognised in the 2004 Tourism Team of the Year Award

The newly re-furbished centre, Spring 2003

A volunteer at work in the osprey centre

The protection hide used by volunteers

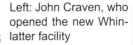

2003 opening in front of the video screen

Left: John Craven, who opened the new Whinlatter facility

Right: Tourism Award

The Lakeland Ospreys

(Continued from page 15)
In 2002 over 100,000 visits were made to the Dodd Wood viewpoint and the Whinlatter Centre CCTV. Ten staff were employed along with over seventy volunteers to inform, advise and enthuse the many visitors to both sites.

As in the previous year, once the juveniles had fledged the nest, the female started to prepare for her migration and took little part in proceedings at the nest. By 24 August she had left. The male continued to fish for the juveniles and took fish to the nest which was regularly visited by the younger birds. All were seen fishing on the lake, but no confirmed sightings were made of the juveniles catching fish for themselves. By 17 September only the male and one juvenile were in the area and by 20 September all the birds had left. The final sighting was of two birds on the 19 September.

Spring 2003 - *Return from migration*

This year the male arrived back first on the 8 April, five days later than last year. The female, by now known to be a 'late bird' returned on the 16 April. She has been very consistent with return dates of 16, 17 twice and 18 April. This affects the breeding season at Bassenthwaite as, mainly due to this late return date, compared with many sites in Scotland, the juveniles and male are still at Bassenthwaite well into September.

Returning from migration

Chris Gomersall rspb-images.com

Excitement was raised on 9 April when a female osprey appeared on the nest and we naturally thought it was 'our' female. It was not to be and, following mating on the nest, this bird was gone the following day. This occurrence did highlight the possibility of migrating female ospreys being cuckolded on passage and potentially not rearing the offspring of the regular mate, or mate of that year. It did, once again, give an indication that the Bassenthwaite valley is a regular migration route for ospreys and this was also noted on 19 and 31 March. Migrating birds, probably mature breeders, are often evident by their strong flight up the lake going north towards Scotland, but always looking for the opportunistic meal below them, a good example of this was early on 2 April when a bird flew north at 0830.

The Lakeland Ospreys

Peregrine intruding at osprey nest site

On 27 April there was much nest making all day with a change of behaviour by the female. She was not seen to eat all day and was very restless with false laying motions. It was on either the evening of the 29 April or early on the 30 April that we believe the first egg was laid, with a second egg on 2 May. It is thought that a third egg may have been laid, but this was never confirmed. The male had a busy day on 3 May. In heavy rain he chased another female osprey from the nest area along with three buzzards.

The incubation times for the pair were similar to previous years with the female sitting for 70% of the time and always at night and the male 28%. The remainder was time with both birds off the nest. An average of fourteen minutes per day was spent off the nest with the eggs uncovered this year. This compares with five minutes per day in 2002 when weather conditions were poor throughout the incubation period.

Intrusions

Various other ospreys were recorded in the area during the summer causing confusion at the viewpoint as to who was who. There was another male in the area for some time. The juvenile mobbed a passing juvenile marsh harrier on 25 August. The second time in three years we have seen this interaction between these species.

It was in mid-August that the breeding female left the area, she was last seen on 17 August. It is always evident when she is preparing to leave, as she fishes for herself once again, visits the nest less regularly and bathes by the lakeshore.

The last sighting of either the male or juvenile was on 9 September. The end of another successful osprey breeding season at Bassenthwaite.

This year was also the first year that the public had access to the newly re-furbished visitor centre at Whinlatter with its live coverage via video link of all of the action on the nest.

The Lakeland Ospreys

Spring 2004 - *Return from migration*

No birds were seen in March this year. The first osprey seen on the lake was on 2 April flying north on migration. Another flew up the east side of the lake on 9 April without stopping.

N Beers-Smith

The 'Bassenthwaite' male was obvious on his return the following day as he arrived straight onto the nest for a quick check before flying down to the lake and onto the 'osprey post' on the shoreline. Sticks were then brought for refurbishment the same day. He did not have to wait long, as the female was back on site on the 14 April at 1920 and again, obviously familiar with the layout of the nest site. Mating began almost immediately with more sticks and moss being brought onto the nest.

Earlier in the day the male had defended the nest from an intruder male presumably on passage. This bird disappeared to the north. On 16 April, however, a further intruder male was in the nest area, which may have been the same bird.

The first egg was laid on the 26 April at 1638, the earliest date so far for this pair. Incubation started almost immediately at 1650.

The following morning the male was on the nest and the female went fishing. One of the few times she would do that until the juvenile had fledged. She caught and returned with a large fish. The second egg was laid on 28 April at 0515.
It was unclear at the time whether a third egg was laid, but this was later proved to be the case when the nest was visited for ringing the juvenile.

A change in behaviour was noted on 4 June and cheeping sounds heard from the nest. A hatch was assumed and confirmed later that day when a chick was fed at 1830. Unfortunately the other eggs failed to hatch and, as in previous years with one chick, the bird developed quickly with the undivided attention of two parents. The two eggs which failed to hatch were sent away for analysis. One was fertile and one was not, but both were clear of any pesticide residue.

The Lakeland Ospreys

As usual, once the female has seen the juvenile fledge the nest (which occurred on 31 July this year) she becomes restless and 'does her own thing' more often and disappears for a while, returns and then migration starts.

This pattern of behaviour occurred once again this year until the last sighting of her on the 15 August.

The juvenile this year was considered a quick learner and it was good to see it catch its own fish for the first time (observed) on 29 August, a good indicator that this bird at least may survive the rigors of the first migration and winter. She/he caught another on 9 September and ate it on the lake shore posts.

By the 13 September both male and juvenile had left.

Spring 2005 - *Return from migration*

The year started on 4 April when the team were in the middle of setting up the protection for the nest area. A message came through that there were two ospreys in the area and immediately a bird landed on the nest. It was subsequently found to be a right leg red ringed bird (Red 02). English and Welsh birds have been colour ringed on the right leg since 2001 with Scottish birds colour ringed on the left leg. Red 02 was quickly checked out through connections with the Rutland Water Osprey Project and confirmed to be a bird translocated from Scotland to Rutland in 2001.

Osprey chick and eggs on nest

Red 02 at Rutland Water

The Lakeland Ospreys

The resident female (Light Green SX) also arrived at the nest and Red 02 tried to attract the attentions of the female by bringing two fish to the nest and attempting to mate. She, however, was lukewarm although she did take the opportunity to grab a fish from him after a fight for it!

The nest had been re-built in February after being blown off in the January storms. It was therefore very encouraging that the new nest design and construction attracted a bird new to the area, the first to arrive and locate it this year.

Nest re-building in 2005

On the 6 April Red 02 was still around and the female was regularly on the nest making a scrape by moving moss on the nest. She seemed to be waiting for her regular partner. What was unclear was what reaction there would be from the usual male to Red 02 and vice versa. Information had come through from Rutland that Red 02 was known to be very aggressive. In the end the usual male arrived back on the 7 April and brought one fish to the nest while Red 02 brought three!

However the intruder read the writing on the wall, as the resident female chose her faithful partner, and Red 02 quickly disappeared without any aggression. He was subsequently seen briefly back at Rutland in May.

Egg laying and osprey Intruders
The rest of the breeding season went off much as previously although a little earlier, with the first egg being laid on 20 April, the

Newly completed nest 2005

The Lakeland Ospreys

second on 23 April and a third egg with the date being unclear, but was either the 26 or 27 April. This third egg was an unmarked white egg without the reddy brown markings usually seen on osprey eggs.

Other ospreys were in the area throughout the summer on at least 25 days, presumably unpaired or immature birds. Reports from other osprey workers indicated that a significant number of birds had encountered problems during migration with strong easterly winds over Spain and Portugal during early April. Many breeders from previous years did not return and others were very late arriving. In the established colonies of Scotland and France there is often a surplus of young adults and these are able to occupy vacant nests, but adverse migratory conditions can very seriously affect newly establishing colonies such as those in England and Wales. We were fortunate that both of the Bassenthwaite birds arrived back on time.

Two of the eggs hatched in 2005. Both juveniles were ringed on 5 July and found, probably, to be a female and a male. Colour rings were fitted as usual (go to page 30 for more information on osprey ringing) which were yellow this year and numbered 34 and 35. The female (Yellow 35) was a very sturdy 1.65kg in weight. It was this bird which developed very quickly and looked strong from fledging to departure. That could not be said for the assumed male (Yellow 34), it weighed 1.35kg.

The female fledged on July 22 at 1520 and looked comparatively competent from the start. We waited until July 27 at 11.11 before the male fledged. By this time the female was flying to and from the nest with ease. However, Yellow 34 caused a great deal of concern to observers as he disappeared for the best part of a week. It was August 2 when he reappeared on the nest looking in poor condition and very hungry. Having presumably been on the forest floor for much of the time it was a wonder he made it back to the nest. The male responded quickly and brought three fish into the nest in the first 20 minutes of the young bird's return! He did gain strength but never filled us with great hope for the future, as he was never seen attempting to fish and looked, at times, to be uncoordinated. He was often to be seen near to or on the nest and constantly begging for food.

Yellow 35 on the other hand was fishing for herself and was seen to catch her own fish on August 13. The adult female, as ever, 'did her own thing', following the fledging and following the provision of a fish to the nest on August 21, she disappeared on migration.

The Lakeland Ospreys

Yellow 35 was not long in following, being last seen flying very high and disappearing on August 25. Generally the male stays in the area until the last juvenile leaves and occasionally provides fish to the nest. The team wondered how long he would stay this year, as Yellow 34 showed no inclination to help himself or to leave the area.

It is unclear if Yellow 34 did leave and we can only assume and hope that he did, but it will only be confirmed if the ring and bird are seen in the future. The last sighting this year, and presumed to be the male, was on September 12.

Osprey pair on the nest (2006)

Spring 2006 - Return from migration

This year the female returned on 3 April and the unringed male, returned on 4 April.

Mating commenced on 4 April at 0920 and ninety four successful mating attempts were recorded up to 23 April when mating ceased.

Three eggs were laid between the 17 and 23 April. The first chick hatched about 2300 on 26 May, was first seen at 0435 on the 27 May and took its first food at 0911. All three chicks had hatched by 29 May.

This was the first time that all three eggs had hatched.

Incubation - In past years the male has undertaken between 28 and 32% (6.25 to 8hrs per day) of the incubation and it was expected that this year would be no different. However, he did less - 25% with a daily average of 6 hours and 2 minutes.

Female on nest

The Lakeland Ospreys

Stick and moss gathering
Up to the end of June 2006 172 sticks were added to the nest; 140 by the male and 32 by the female.

Intruders in 2006
The most common intruders are buzzards and crows. However a peregrine was seen on one day and a goshawk on three days. Other ospreys were seen on at least 18 days visiting the nest site and there were at least 23 days when other ospreys were viewed from Dodd wood viewpoint.

On 20 May a visiting osprey actually landed on the nest! No rings were seen.

Osprey carrying moss for nest building

Ringing
The three chicks were ringed and measured on the morning of 5 July.

Fledgings
The first chick (5Z) flew on Thursday 20 July at 1435, the second chick on Saturday 22 July and the last one took to the air on Sunday 23 July 2006.

Chick Green 5Z having his ring fitted

A 2006 chick having its wing measured

The Lakeland Ospreys

The Osprey Year

The osprey year, as far as the Lake District Osprey Project is concerned, starts in April when they return to the UK from wintering in Africa. The majority are just passing through on their way to Northern Scotland with its forests containing flat-topped Scots pines; ideal nesting sites for these birds. In 2001 one pair decided to end their journey at Bassenthwaite and take up residence in Cumbria. Now this may partly be due to the fact that the osprey population is increasing (there are now over 180 known breeding pairs in Scotland), but the main reason must surely be the provision of several artificial nests in Whinlatter forest. The foresight of a few enthusiasts and the co-operation of interested organisations and many individuals, both employed and volunteers have brought this about.

Tree climbers at the Bassenthwaite osprey Nest

1.   Providing the osprey with an attractive home

Bassenthwaite at first sight has almost everything that an osprey pair would require to bring up a family. There is a large freshwater lake with an abundance of suitable fish and adjacent forests within sight and easy reach of the lake. However Whinlatter is a relatively small recreational forest, open to the public and the venue for a variety of recreational activities. The osprey is a shy bird during the breeding season and will not stand close human approach and the local conifers do not generally provide the sort of flat open platform required for an osprey nest.

This was recognised by local 'birders' and so in 1998 the first artificial nest sites were built (see page 7-9 and 22). This was possible because of the expertise of the Lake District National Park Authority tree climbers, two of whom are seen in these photographs.

Once the ospreys have arrived, paired and chosen their nest site the next stage in the osprey year is taken up with mating, feeding, and protecting their territory, prior to incubating and then rearing their young. This has already been described in some detail for the 2003 ospreys (see pages 18-19).

Osprey in a tree with a pike

2.   Fishing to feed oneself and the family

The male undertakes virtually all the fishing throughout the breeding period, the female remaining on or near the nest. Our male is a very proficient fisherman and often catches a fish on the first or second attempts. The average noted in previous studies has been one fish for four attempts for experienced birds. Our male is either very proficient, or the lake has a good supply of fish in shallow water. It is probably a combination of both.

The head is bitten off before presenting the fish to the female

He flies over the lake at 80 metres, hovers with feet hanging if a fish is seen and drops to within a metre of the surface. If successful he rises from the surface, shaking off water in flight. The fish is always carried head first in either one or two feet, the special reversible claw located for best grip. The head is usually eaten off by the male before the fish is presented to the female at the nest during incubation. Fish caught tend to be in the region of up to 500 grams.

Bassenthwaite is rich in fish species, including Britain's rarest, the Vendace (a deep-water dweller not normally available to an osprey!) and over ten other species.

For the osprey, an opportunist, anything swimming near the surface is fair game and observers have noted Perch ,Roach,

Osprey going fishing

The osprey usually carries its prey with the head forward.

The Lakeland Ospreys

Pike, Eel and Trout being caught. These are rich pickings indeed compared to the osprey heartland of Speyside where only three species tend to dominate the diet. A 240g roach and the remains of a 500g perch have been found on the Bassenthwaite nest. The table on page 5 shows the percentage of different fish seen to be caught by the Bassenthwaite ospreys since 2004.

3. Ringing and measuring the chicks before they fledge

Once all the chicks are hatched and appear to be in good health at about 5 to 6 weeks of age they are ready to be ringed. On ringing day the weather has to be dry and not too windy. At about 5 a.m. the team gathers and approaches the nest with the aim of removing the chicks from the nest, carrying out the ringing and replacing them as quickly as possible - usually well within one hour from start to finish.

At the nest site the climbing team climb immediately up the tree to the nest. Here they set up a roping system to ensure the chicks are lowered safely one by one in a canvas bag to the ringing team on the ground, Pete Davies and Peter Baron. The chicks are ringed, measured (see also page 25) and weighed. These results are recorded for future reference. Bassenthwaite chicks normally have their identification number, a coloured ring, placed on the right leg so that they can easily be distinguised from a distance from the Scottish chicks, who have the identification number on the left leg. Along with the detailed measurements the chicks are photographed, because the face and head markings remain the

The tools needed for ringing and measuring the chicks

Bringing the chicks down from the nest in a canvas bag, one at a time

Removing the chick from the bag

same for life and birds can be identified by these alone, given good views.

Chick having a ring fitted

The first time three chicks have fledged from the nest

Weighing the chick using a spring balance

4. Preparing for migration
Once the chicks are fledged the female osprey feeds and rests prior to migration. She invariably leaves well before her partner (always by mid-August). The male stays on, catching and taking fish to the nest, until the last of the juveniles leave. He is usually the last of the family to depart.

5. The Future
With osprey populations increasing, chicks leaving Cumbria and provision of more nest platforms, the hope is that the Cumbria osprey population will also expand over the coming years. All involved in the Lake District Osprey Project hope so!

The Lakeland Ospreys

J Baptiste Pons